HOW TO BE
CONTENT

HOW TO BE CONTENT

An inspired guide to happiness

Lona Eversden & Dr. Arlene K. Unger

Illustrations by Joanne Parry

WHITE LION
PUBLISHING

CONTENTS

SEEKING HAPPINESS

Happiness is the ultimate life goal for most people. Yet the majority of us have no idea how to achieve it, or even what it really is. We might think that we want more money, a bigger house, a better job — but the reality of all those things is that they tend to bring only short-term pleasure before we grow hungry for something bigger and better, and so find ourselves discontent once more. True happiness is an attitude of mind that all of us can cultivate, no matter where or how we are living. It is a way of being rather than a goal; a journey rather than a destination.

But how do we become more content? This is a conundrum that people have always grappled with. What we do know is that, so long as the basics of life are in place and we are no longer struggling for survival, humans strive for meaning, worth and joy. Down the ages thinkers and writers, poets and artists have tried to get to the root of happiness — some have made it their life's work. More widely, people throughout history and across cultures have happened on their own recipe for contentment and passed it on like a family heirloom. Insights into happy living are embedded like fossils in our shared cultural heritage — myths and legends, proverbs and sayings, celebrations and festivals, and in the symbols and icons of myriad spiritual beliefs, traditions and customs.

So the signposts to happiness are all around us, if only we can recognize them for what they are. If we are attentive and attuned, we can benefit from the deep and universal wisdom that is a part of

*'Folks are usually about as happy as they
make their minds up to be.'*

ABRAHAM LINCOLN

every country and every tradition in the world. After all, modern research has already shown that, despite all technological and social advancement, we tap into the same deep roots of happiness that our ancestors did: it exists in family, friendship and community, in good health, meaningful work and the sense of transcendence that can come from engagement with higher things such as art, spiritual beliefs, music, literature and philanthropy. These are the things that make life worth living, and they are a real source of joy.

Be Inspired

In this book, we take a meandering journey through the rich philosophical landscape of contentment. Along the way, we encounter universal or common symbols of joy, such as the sun and the bluebird, and explore ideas about happiness through Norse mythology, Persian folklore, Scandinavian lifestyle, Buddhist teachings, the philosophy of Ancient Greece and Rome, as well as the work of great artists and poets.

'There is no duty we so much underrate as the duty of being happy. By being happy we sow anonymous benefits upon the world.'

ROBERT LOUIS STEVENSON

Each symbol, myth or idea is expounded through a short text or a traditional tale, and each one leads on to a practical exercise or set of tips that can inspire greater satisfaction or happiness in your everyday life. This is a book that you can dip into occasionally as a way of finding inspiration, or that you can use as a practical guide for life. Either way, you will be exploring ancient wisdom that is backed up with modern psychological understanding and research. Of course, some ideas or techniques will strike a chord with you more than others — and that is good. Research shows that we are more likely to keep up a new habit if it is something that we enjoy, so start with the ideas that draw you most and then widen your horizons and try something different.

Wisdom from All Sources

The book is divided into four chapters. The first deals with The Natural World, because humankind has always found uplifting significance in the majesty of the landscape and the cycle of the seasons. Chapter Two looks at Cultures Around the World and how societies down the ages and across the globe have approached the universal quest for contentment. In the third chapter, Mythology & Folklore, we look at the legends and stories that point the way to the well-lived life. The fourth and final chapter, Philosophers, Writers & Poets, explores the insights into contentment that have come to us from some of history's greatest minds.

Happiness is elusive, it is true, but it is not illusory. Whatever your past or your current circumstances, however you feel and wherever you are headed, you have the opportunity to become a happier more joyful person and find contentment in every day.

CHAPTER ONE:

THE NATURAL WORLD

❯❮❯❮

'There is a pleasure in the pathless woods,
There is a rapture on the lonely shore,
There is society, where none intrudes,
By the deep sea, and music in its roar:
I love not man the less, but Nature more.'

LORD BYRON

A BRIGHT NEW DAY

As the pre-eminent source of life-giving energy, illumination and warmth, the sun symbolizes positivity, vitality and joyfulness. Since ancient times, people have recognized the power of the sun and have invented stories to explain its passage across the sky, its rising and setting, its relationship with the darkness and the moon. Advanced civilizations, such as the Greeks, Romans and Egyptians, recognized it as a source of power and used it as a symbol of authority and kingship.

Gods of Light

All ancient belief systems contain stories about the sun, but none are more complex or varied than those of the Greeks. In their mythology Apollo, a kind of divine poet, was the god of creativity and sunlight. He was known by epithets such as *Aegletes*, 'the light of the sun', *Phanaeus*, 'the giver of light', and *Phoebus*, 'brightly shining'. The sun itself, meanwhile, was personified as Helios. Every morning, Helios emerged from the east, driving a golden chariot drawn by fire-breathing horses. Each day's ride would end in the western land of the Hesperides, and the horses of Helios would rest on the Blessed Isles, where they grazed on magic herbs. As a god of light, Helios was considered to be all-knowing and all-seeing — and so, to the modern mind, he stands for the gift of self-awareness that is an integral part of happiness.

'The bright sun, that brings back,
not light alone, but new life, and
hope, and freshness to man.'

CHARLES DICKENS,
OLIVER TWIST

BASK IN THE LIGHT

'Keep your face always toward the sunshine —
and the shadows will fall behind you.'

WALT WHITMAN

Scientists are discovering that natural daylight is key to our well-being. One American study found that people who worked near a window were more active and slept better than those in windowless offices. Another study, from Cornell University, discovered that nurses working near natural light were not only more alert but they laughed more and were nicer to patients than colleagues who spent their shift in mostly artificial light. So, as a simple way to lift your mood, bring more light into your life.

1. If it is light when you wake up, throw open the blinds or curtains straight away and spend a few moments looking out of the window. Maximize the amount of natural light in your home and try to gravitate towards the window when you are doing something like reading or crafts.

2. Spend time outdoors every lunchtime. Exposure to daylight helps boost levels of feel-good serotonin in the body, so is a natural mood lifter.

3. Find something you like doing outdoors — this is easy if you enjoy team sports or running, or if you like gardening. If not, then try incorporating walking

into your journey to work – perhaps by getting off a stop earlier or by parking further away from your destination. Persuade friends to meet for a walk rather than a coffee, find an outdoor t'ai chi class, or sit and watch the world go by from a bench in a park.

SUNSHINE VITAMIN

Natural light triggers the body's production of vitamin D (the sunshine vitamin), a lack of which has been connected to depression. So if you are feeling low, try upping the time you spend outside.

THE GARDENER'S HELPMATE

The brilliant scarlet coat of the ladybird is a cheery sight, and many traditions around the world link this little beetle with good fortune and happy events. Most cultures hold that it is unlucky to kill one; a Swedish superstition says if a ladybird lands on a young woman's hand it signals that she will soon be married, Austrians consider them a portent of good weather, the Chinese believe it fortuitous to find a ladybird in the home, and an old English superstition says that ladybirds carry off illness when they fly away.

By Any Other Name

The world over, this beautiful little creature has a colourful, interesting and often religious name. One English tale holds that once a swarm of aphids invaded the fields. Worried for their harvest, countryfolk prayed to Our Lady, the Virgin Mary, for her help. A host of scarlet-cloaked little beetles appeared and devoured the pests, saving the ripening crops. The beetles were dubbed 'Our Lady's bird' in the Virgin's honour. Other European languages also make an honorific link with Mary. In German, a ladybird is a *Marienkäfer*, a 'Mary-beetle'; and in Spain it is *mariquita*, a 'Little Mary'. In other languages, God himself – and animals other than birds – are invoked. Russian for ladybird is *bozhya korovka*, 'God's little cow'. The French dialect term *vache à dieu* means the same thing, though in some parts of France a ladybird is a *poulette de la Madone* – Madonna's chicken.

'This lucky little ladybug
Has landed here to stay,
To make my garden pretty
And keep the weeds away.'

UNKNOWN

MINDFUL GARDENING

'One who plants a garden plants happiness.'
CHINESE PROVERB

Take inspiration from the ladybird and get out into the garden —
spending time here could be the secret to feeling happier. One UK
study found that 80 per cent of gardeners proclaimed themselves
satisfied with life (compared with 67 per cent of non-gardeners),
while a US study of 600 gardeners discovered that five hours or
more a week spent tending the garden led to a significant increase
in contentment. In fact, there is so much evidence to show that
gardening can make us happy that some doctors are recommending
it as a form of therapy to patients with depression. Here's how to
introduce a little ecotherapy into your life.

Be here now   When you garden, focus all your attention on what
you are doing, moment by moment. Gift yourself this time to be
truly present.

Let go of judgement   Don't worry about how good you are at
gardening, or your previous successes or failures. Decide on a task
and do it methodically and without an internal commentary.

Be deadline-free   Enjoy being in the garden for as long as feels right
for you — it could be ten minutes, it could be a couple of hours.
There's no need to watch the clock.

Go by instinct You don't need a degree in design to create a beautiful garden. Enjoy the process of going by instinct, deciding to move that pot here or plant this shrub there.

Indulge the senses Become aware of the colours and patterns around you; breathe in the aromas; note the textures of the plants; hear the sounds of the birds and insects; and allow yourself to taste any fruit or vegetables you grow straight from the ground or the tree.

Get your hands dirty Soil contains a bacterium that is thought to trigger the release of the feel-good hormone serotonin — yet another reason why gardening gives us a boost.

Grow your own There's nothing more joyous than the sight of your own home-grown produce — scientists have found that harvesting your own fruit or vegetables can give you a mini-high.

Pause and be Don't feel you need to be constantly working; stop from time to time and enjoy this beautiful moment. Stand and watch the ladybird in flight or at rest, or marvel at some of the many other creatures that make their home in the garden.

FOOD FOR THE SOUL

'Divide an orange — it tastes just as good.'

CHINESE PROVERB

We all know that it is good to eat fruit and vegetables for our health, but did you know they can also make you feel happier? A study of more than 12,000 people by the University of Queensland, Australia, and the University of Warwick in the UK found that people felt happier with every piece of fruit or vegetable they added to their daily diet, up to eight portions a day. So it's official: eating healthily is good for your mood. Here are other foodie tips that help your happiness levels.

Go natural Generally speaking, the closer a food is to its natural state, the better it is for you. Keep foods that are highly processed to a minimum.

Be complex Carbohydrates, like rice and potatoes, help to increase the amount of the feel-good chemical serotonin in the brain. That's why we turn to crisps and pastries when we need a lift. But the effect doesn't last long and our mood crashes back down. Go for complex carbs – wholegrains such as oats or brown rice – which have a much slower serotonin effect.

Drink water Keeping hydrated helps to regulate your mood. If you find yourself feeling snappy or tired, try drinking a glass of water and see if that helps. Avoid having too much caffeine, especially after lunch, because it affects sleep and can make you jittery.

Eat regularly Skipping meals can have a big effect on your mood. Eating breakfast means you are less likely to reach for a sugary snack mid-morning; if you don't have time for lunch, go for a couple of smaller meals evenly spaced throughout the day.

Oranges are symbols of happiness and
abundance in China, because their brilliant
colour and round form is reminiscent of the sun.

THE BLUEBIRD OF HAPPINESS

The charming bluebird is an enduring symbol of joy worldwide. The deep blue of its plumage recalls the heavens – and so the promise of eternal happiness in many legends. For many Native Americans, the bluebird is an important symbol of spring and transition, and its beautiful song is considered to be the herald of spring (like the cuckoo's call in Europe). The Navajo people link the bluebird's song to the dawn, the daily rather than the yearly return to light and warmth. In European fairy tales, the bluebird appears as a symbol of hope and as a reminder that true happiness lies in the simple pleasures of life, which are there for all of us if only we can realize it.

Symbol of Happiness

The modern-day popularity of the bluebird stems from Maurice Maeterlinck's play *The Blue Bird* in 1908, which was based on a French story in which two children are sent on a journey to find the bluebird of happiness. They face many perils and ultimately fail in their quest – until they return home and discover that the bluebird was in their possession all along, in the form of a pet bird. The hopeful message that happiness is always within our grasp made the play hugely popular and it inspired seven films, a children's novel and an opera. The American song 'Bluebird of Happiness' followed in 1934. In the same decade two other hugely popular songs – 'Over the Rainbow' and 'The White Cliffs of Dover' – mention bluebirds as symbols of the hope for happiness.

APPRECIATING SMALL PLEASURES

Is our happiness really in our grasp, as the tale of *The Blue Bird* suggests? In lots of ways it is, because no matter how tricky our current situation may be, it is always possible to appreciate what we have and find moments of contentment in the simplest of things. The fact is that most of us go through the motions as we go about our day, so we miss out on many of the tiny joys that are already a part of it. If only we could live more in the moment.

A cup of joy Spend five minutes in the morning savouring a cup of tea or coffee – or a glass of water. Simply let go of the need to do anything else while you are drinking and appreciate each sip.

Time to pause Arrive a few minutes early when you are meeting a friend or have an appointment. Leave your phone in your bag or pocket, and use this time to sit, breathe, and look around you.

Beauty all around Make a point of finding something beautiful to appreciate every day on your journey to work – a pretty flower or shrub, the smile of a passer-by, an interesting building. If you really can't find anything, vary your route to work!

Looking up We get used to looking slightly down as we walk along. Every now and then, stop and look up the sky – remind yourself that the world is bigger than you.

Hold hands There's a reason that we instinctively do this in times of troubles — it reduces stress. And holding hands with someone you care about is a great way to reconnect.

Voice thanks When you get a compliment, say thank you. If someone holds a door open for you, or lets you go ahead of them, acknowledge it. Once you are on the lookout, you will realize that you are the recipient of many small acts of kindness every day.

'The bluebird carries the sky on his back.'

HENRY DAVID THOREAU

BEE HAPPY

'How doth the little busy Bee
Improve each shining hour,
And gather honey all the day
From ev'ry op'ning flow'r!'

ISAAC WATTS

A bee flies up to 10 miles (16km) a day to collect pollen and nectar for the hive, heading out over and over again in search of new, untapped flowers. It is estimated that more than two million flowers are visited to make a single pound (454g) of honey. Thus the bee has rightly come to represent hard work, while the hive, with its strict social structure and well-organized community, has come to epitomize togetherness and working for the common good, both of which have been found to be an integral part of a happy life.

Melissa

Melissa is the scientific name for the bee, as well as the name of a mountain-nymph in Greek myth. In one version of her story, Melissa discovers honeycomb and introduces it to mankind; in another, she also saves the baby Zeus from his murderous father, feeding him honey to help him thrive. Melissa is transformed into an earthworm as a punishment for defying the evil deity, but Zeus, who later becomes king of the gods, turns her into the bee so she can continue to reap the sweet reward of good deeds.

VOLUNTEER FOR HAPPINESS

There is something very appealing about the unselfish work ethic of the bee — and it is a character trait worth emulating. Doing things for the good of others gives you a 'helper's high'. It seems that this kind of altruism activates the part of our brain connected to a sense of reward and pleasure. Volunteering also allows you to engage with your community, which is linked to greater life satisfaction. You don't have to devote huge amounts of time and energy either — every little helps — but one study by researchers at the London School of Economics found that the more people volunteered, the happier they were. Here's how to make the most of volunteering:

Love what you do Giving because you feel you have to can be counterproductive, so try to volunteer both in a way that feels enjoyable and for a cause you believe in. For example, if you are passionate about animals, then helping in a rescue centre might be a perfect fit for you; if you enjoy gardening, then perhaps a local hospital or park needs people to help maintain the grounds.

Work your way Do you love the camaraderie of a team, or prefer to achieve things on your own? Or would you prefer to volunteer with a friend to make it more enjoyable?

Open your mind Volunteering can allow you to learn new skills or try new things, so don't be too rigid about what you do.

FIND YOUR PLACE

There are all kinds of ways to find volunteering opportunities:
ring an organization that you want to support or check out
their website, contact your local government office or search
'how to volunteer in [your local area]' on the Internet. And
be prepared to persevere: voluntary organizations are often
short-staffed so may take a while to get back to you.

Make a commitment Be realistic about how much time you have to
volunteer — two hours a week, one afternoon a month — and stick
to it. If an ad-hoc arrangement suits you better, find an occasional
opportunity such as a beach clean.

Factor in the travel time A lengthy journey to an organization may
tip the balance in favour of one that is closer to home. Do what
makes volunteering feel easy and fun.

Be prepared to learn Ask questions when you need to, take notes,
shadow an experienced volunteer. You'll get far more out of a
volunteering experience when you know what you are doing.

'Be thou the rainbow in the storms of life. The
evening beam that smiles the clouds away, and tints
tomorrow with prophetic ray.'

LORD BYRON

RAIN AND SHINE

The iridescent rainbow has long been associated with optimism and is a promise of contentment after a period of difficulty, because it is a result of sunshine after rain. Evidence shows that an attitude of hope pays dividends when it comes to your overall contentment, and the good news is that you can train yourself to become more optimistic. Next time you are feeling overwhelmed or negative, ask yourself these three simple questions to help shift your attitude towards the positive end of the spectrum.

How long will this issue last? If you have a problem, consider how long it is going to affect you. Be realistic and avoid exaggeration. An optimist will recognize that the difficulty will shift in time.

How much of my life is affected? It's easy to see a single issue or problem as pervading everything and stopping you from doing anything you enjoy. Optimists acknowledge that one situation is only part of a whole. Challenge yourself to find positive things in your life that remain unaffected.

How can I help myself? You may not be able to fix every problem, but think what will help with your current situation – this may mean being patient and allowing events to unfold, it may involve positive action, or it may mean focusing on taking care of yourself so that you are better able to cope. Often you'll find that releasing the need to end or fix a situation will in itself open up new possibilities.

SOARING ASPIRATIONS

The image of a majestic mountain, with its peak reaching into the sky, has always been linked to a desire for higher understanding — spiritual aspiration — and climbing a mountain a way of showing devotion, a metaphor for the personal journey towards spiritual realization. It is for this reason that many monasteries and shrines are built into mountainsides and at their summits.

The Tale of Mount Fuji

Fuji in Japan is a perfect mountain to look on: its slopes form a symmetrical triangle, its peak is crowned with snow, it stands in isolation — no lesser peak obstructs its profile. An active volcano, Fuji was seen as a sacred mountain by the Ainu, the ancient inhabitants of Japan, and it is possible that its name derives from their word for a god of fire. Legend has it that the cone-shaped mountain was created in a single day. In one tale, a woodcutter hears a huge boom and runs away in terror, believing it to be an earthquake. On his return, he discovers that the flat area around his hut has become a mountain, which he names 'the never-dying mountain' — Fujiyama. The mountain became viewed as the sacred home of several deities, including the Shinto goddess Sengen whose shrine at the mountain's peak has become a site of pilgrimage. Legend holds that only the devout can make it — less worthy pilgrims are thrown from the mountain by the goddess. Thus reaching the summit represents both fulfilment and purity.

REACH YOUR GOALS

'Climb the mountains and get their good tidings.
Nature's peace will flow into you as sunshine flows into trees.'
JOHN MUIR

Living a life of contentment includes being successful at setting and accomplishing goals. Just like the mountaineer who sets out to reach Sengen's shrine at the peak of Mount Fuji, we need to find our purpose and direction. Goals enable us to look forward to challenges, overcome obstacles and realize our potential. Being content means that you are always in the mode of strengthening, improving and evolving. If you are feeling uninspired, here are a few goal-setting tips to adopt:

Attitude   Missing out on opportunities or not creating them only leads to more discontentment. Create a positive attitude by seeking out people or things that will support your growth, as well as ways that you can help support others to achieve their own goals. Gradually you will feel more supported and capable of making your vision happen.

Authenticity   Being truly genuine can help us connect with others and ultimately be happier. Give yourself permission to 'just be you' and notice how much you feel a part of life. The more you are true to your own values, the more life will seem interesting, purposeful and content.

Acceptance Unrealistic expectations tend to lead to disappointment. Accepting the natural progress of things makes life sweeter. Allowing yourself to accept who you are and what you have been given now can give the impetus to meet any goal.

Ability Comparing yourself to others only eats away at our own unique skills and self-esteem. Believing in your abilities and starting each day with an 'I can' will point you in the best direction for success.

THE ENCHANTED FOREST

'Trees are poems that the earth writes upon the sky.'

KAHLIL GIBRAN

T he forest appears in countless fairy tales and myths as a place of magic and mystery, and forest or tree worship was prevalent in many ancient cultures. In prehistoric times when men were hunter-gatherers, the forest played an important role as a place of safety and sanctuary, and it is often depicted as such a refuge in folklore — think of Robin Hood hiding out in the impenetrable depths of Sherwood and the Hindu love story of Rama and Sita.

Forests are commonly seen as a symbol of the unconscious, and being lost in or exploring the forest appears in many stories as a way of suggesting a rite of passage or some kind of necessary internal progress on the pathway to happiness.

Retreat and Reflection

The idea of the forest as a place of introspection and reflection comes up often in Buddhism. The Buddha himself spent many years wandering through forests, and it is no coincidence that he found enlightenment while sitting under a tree. He encouraged his followers to dwell in forests because they induce calm and mental focus. Even today there are many forest monasteries in Thailand, where monks can live as simply as the Buddha did more than 2,500 years ago.

FOREST BATHING

'The clearest way into the Universe is through a forest wilderness.'

JOHN MUIR

Developed in Japan in the 1980s, 'forest bathing' is the beautiful practice of spending time in the woods. Our society has become reliant on technology, and at the same time cut off from the natural world — but there are countless studies to show that connecting with nature is linked to greater happiness and well-being. A study in Berlin even found that the part of the brain that processes fear and stress (the amygdala) was healthier in people who lived within a kilometre of a forest. To help soothe your spirits and promote feelings of happiness, take a forest bath...

1. Go to an area of forest or woodland. Switch off all gadgets and place them at the bottom of your bag or in your car. Better yet, leave them at home.
2. Walk into the forest and immerse yourself in the sights and sounds, the woody textures and the earthy smells. Let go of any need to arrive at a destination; give yourself up to the experience of being.
3. When you feel you want to, stop for a while under a tree — feel its trunk, notice the leaves and other details, perhaps the plants underneath it.

4. Sit and enjoy the experience of being in the forest for a while. When you feel you want to, get up and walk again.

5. Breathe deeply — not only is deep breathing good for you, but forest air contains substances (phytoncides) emitted by the trees and plants that promote better immune systems.

6. Spend at least half an hour in the forest — a couple of hours is even better — before making your way out.

———————— ⌒⌒⌒⌒⌒ ————————

SOOTHING THE BODY

A Japanese study found that spending thirty minutes in a forest environment reduced the level of the stress hormone cortisol in the body, lowered the pulse rate and blood pressure, and increased the activity of the parasympathetic nerve activity, which promotes rest, while reducing activity of the sympathetic nervous system, which controls the stress response.

———————— ⌒⌒⌒⌒⌒ ————————

LETTING GO

Poets and writers throughout the ages have reflected on the beauty of autumn, that 'bright solemn fading of the year' as Elizabeth Gaskell called it in her novel *Wives and Daughters*. Autumn is the perfect symbol of natural endings and of letting go; as we watch the leaves fall from the trees, this can inspire us to release things and attitudes that no longer serve us, making room for new experiences. Try this exercise if feelings about the past are holding you back from embracing contentment in the present.

1. Take a pebble, pine cone or other small non-breakable object that you can comfortably fit in your hand.
2. Think of the issue that is holding you back — perhaps old resentment or anger, jealousy, regret or shame. Imagine the object in your hand represents this emotion.
3. Use your fingers to roll the object over your hand, noticing that it is not attached to you and can easily be moved. When you feel ready, open your hand, turn it over and let the object fall to the ground.
4. If the emotion resurfaces, you can visualize yourself doing this — simply letting go and allowing the feeling to drop away from you.

'Seasons of mists and mellow fruitfulness'

JOHN KEATS

WINGING IT

'Reflected in the dragonfly's eye — mountains.'

KOBAYASHI ISSA

The beautiful dragonfly is a symbol of transformation and adaptability, since it begins its life in the water and then undergoes a metamorphosis so that it can fly through the air. Seeming light and insubstantial, it is able to fly long distances by gliding on the wind. Thus, the dragonfly provides an inspirational example of how it is sometimes possible to make progress by accepting rather than struggling against circumstance, reminding us to embrace change.

Magical Creatures

In many European cultures the dragonfly has a sinister symbolism, but the Native Americans see it as a symbol of happiness and speed. It is the emblem of Japan, which is known as the Island of the Dragonfly because — legend has it — the island and nearby mainland resemble two dragonflies mating when viewed from above. The swift flight of the dragonfly, together with its excellent hunting skills, have endowed it with the name 'victory insect' (*kachimushi*), and it was adopted as a totem by samurai warriors as a reminder never to give up. Dragonfly symbols appear frequently in Japanese art because of this association.

ACCEPTING CHANGE

In many civilizations, the dragonfly symbolizes adaptability to change – and change is something that we all have to deal with in life, whether it is starting a new job, relocating home or losing a loved one. Psychologists have discovered that people who are adaptable to change have greater contentment then those who are resistant to new circumstances. For times when you feel overwhelmed by change, or uncertain about shifting circumstances in your life, use this exercise to encourage a more positive outlook.

1. Turn your attention to how your life was a month ago and where it is now. How many new things have come into your life? It may only be something small, such as a new exercise class you enjoy or route to work you have discovered, or something larger – a new job, relationship or hobby.

2. Reflect on how these changes have impacted you for the better – the excitement, opportunities or joy that have stemmed from these additions to your life.

3. Keeping that positive attitude at the forefront of your mind, reflect on any changes on the horizon that have been causing you anxiety. Consider adopting a new approach towards these potential changes: what are the opportunities that they offer? How will they positively impact your life for the better? Remember that for every downside there is most likely an upside: a challenging

situation at work might prompt us to learn new skills, even a disruption to your commute may present a chance to finish that chapter of your book.

4. Begin to think of change as something that can turn lethargy into action. Maybe your company is relocating away from your favorite gym — an opportunity to try another way of working out. What if your adult children move away? That could inspire you to travel more and discover a new area. Seeing unexpected change as a helpful agent for progress encourages us accept it more.

5. Remember all the positive things that have come into your life in the past month as a result of change and close the exercise by practicing gratitude for these blessings in your life.

GUIDING LIGHT

Humankind has always been mesmerized by the brilliant stars in the night sky. They are symbols of divine light in the darkness and are linked to the idea of spiritual enlightenment or ultimate happiness. In Jewish tradition, the six-pointed star — the Star of David — is a symbol of protection; for Christians, the same symbol is often associated with the Star of Bethlehem, which presaged the joyful, hopeful birth of the saviour-king.

Morning and Night

The brightest object in the sky after the sun and moon is the morning star — which is actually not a star at all, but the planet Venus. When the astronomical conditions are right, it appears briefly in the eastern morning sky before sunrise and again in the western evening sky at dusk. For a time, the Greeks believed that the morning and evening stars were separate objects in the heavens and gave them separate names. The Australian Yolngu people call the planet Venus 'Banumbirr' and describe how this deity guided the first people to Australia from the east. They celebrate Banumbirr's rising with a ceremony before dawn; the star is said to appear drawing a rope of light behind her, along which the people of the earth can send messages to departed loved ones. The light from stars takes years or centuries to reach us, and so we see them as they were long, long ago. For this reason, they can symbolize remembrance of loved ones or things past.

NOSTALGIA AND HAPPINESS

'The evening star is the most beautiful of all.'

SAPPHO

There's much emphasis these days about being in the present. And although it is true that being in the moment can make us feel happy, there is also place for active nostalgia. A study by the University of Southampton found that looking back over happy memories helped promote optimism and positive feelings of self-esteem. Why? Because remembering happy times gives us psychological comfort, promotes positive feelings of belonging and reminds us that life can be meaningful and pleasurable. Here's how to use nostalgia as a feel-good therapy.

QUICK FIX

Try putting on some music that reminds you of your childhood or a happy period of your life. It's an easy nostalgia fix that can lift your mood in an instant.

---

1. Get comfortable and softly close your eyes. Think of a happy memory from your childhood or an earlier part of your life.
2. If you find this hard, then consider a festival that you celebrate and is important to you – Christmas, Eid, Divali, Thanksgiving – or a favourite pastime, and see if that triggers a good memory.
3. Try to remember the event in as much detail as you can – where you were, who you were with, what you ate or did. Do this for as long as feels right.
4. If any sad or difficult memories surface, try to let them be. Memories are often bittersweet, but allow yourself the pleasure of reliving the good bits.
5. Try writing a paragraph on the event in your journal. Often you'll find that more details come flooding back once you put pen to paper.

A PLACE TO REST

'There is some of the same fitness in a man's building his own house
that there is in a bird's building its own nest.'

HENRY DAVID THOREAU

Although our happiness is made up of many factors, including our relationships, community connections, job security and the like, a study of 8,000 Britons concluded that sleep is the single most important aspect of a healthy lifestyle when it comes to feeling contented. Every creature needs a place to feel safe so they can rest, and here's how to create a nest that promotes a good night's sleep.

Go dark   We are hard-wired to sleep at night: darkness promotes the production of melanin, the hormone that promotes sleep. Use thick curtains or blackout blinds to make your room as dark as you can, or use an eye mask. Thick curtains will also help muffle unwelcome noise from outdoors.

Keep electronics out   Keep your mobile downstairs so you are not tempted to look at it at bedtime – electronic screens emit a blue light that interferes with the body's natural inclination to sleep at night. For the same reason, read a paper book rather than an e-reader and avoid having an alarm clock with a bright digital display on your bedside table.

Soothe yourself Make your bedroom a place of calm by using soft colours, plenty of touch-friendly fabrics and beautiful objects that make you feel happy when you look at them. Keep anything to do with work out — along with any exercise equipment and the TV.

Have a ritual Spend the period before bedtime doing activities that make you feel happy and relaxed. You may like to have a warm bath, light a scented candle, practise meditation or relaxation techniques or listen to soft music. Make the hour before bed a time that promotes rest.

CHAPTER TWO:
CULTURES AROUND
THE WORLD

*'Every object, every being,
is a jar full of delight.'*

RUMI

IN HARMONY

T he yin-yang symbol indicates much more than happiness; the intertwined light and dark halves of a circle are a beautiful evocation of perfect balance. Rooted in Chinese mythology from at least the third century BCE, this deceptively simple symbol embodies a complex view of the world. It is a visual expression of the idea that the universe is made up of opposing forces: energies that are in a constant state of flux as one gives way to the other. And yet, since each contains the other at its centre, they are interdependent, inseparable, in a dynamic state of equilibrium. Chinese thought holds that the universe and everything in it contains both yin and yang energy, and one cannot exist without the other.

The Birth of Yin Yang

Yin represents the earth, feminine energy, receptiveness, passivity and darkness, while yang stands for the heavens, masculine energy, activity and light. They are traditionally thought of in terms of sunlight moving across a mountain — one side of the mountain is bathed in brightness and is warm and dry (this is yang, which can be translated as 'sunny side'), while the other is in shade, so is damp and cold (yin, meaning 'shady side'). As the sun moves across the sky, the light progresses from one side to the other, always in motion, until the dark side becomes light and the light becomes dark.

'All things carry yin and embrace yang. They reach
harmony by blending with the vital breath.'

LAO TZU

LIFTING THE SKY

'The interplay of opposite principles constitutes the universe.'
CONFUCIUS

The concept of yin yang lies at the heart of Chinese medicine and of healing practices such as t'ai chi and qigong, which aim to keep yin and yang energy flowing through the body to promote good health. Many studies have found that t'ai chi and qigong engender feelings of well-being, as well as bringing significant health benefits. Try this well-known qigong exercise for a quick happiness boost when you are feeling low.

1. Stand with your feet flat on the floor and roughly hip width apart, toes pointing forwards. Your spine should be upright and your chin roughly parallel to the floor. Bend your knees slightly as if about to sit on a tall bar stool.
2. Take a few deep breaths in this position, allowing your body to relax.
3. Bring your hands in front of your belly, with your palms facing downwards and your fingertips of each hand pointing towards the other. Keep your hands relaxed rather than rigidly straight; there should be a little space in between each finger.
4. Looking down at your hands, raise them in an arc in front of the body and then above the head as you take a long slow breath in. Follow the movement of the hands

STAND TALL

This exercise is great for your posture, and a study by
the University of Auckland has found that good posture
helps to alleviate the symptoms of depression.

with your eyes, bringing your head up to facilitate this
— only lift the head as far as feels comfortable; don't
compress the neck.

5. At the end of this upward arc, when your palms are
facing the sky, raise them straight up a little — as if
'pressing the sky'. Keep the action very soft and gentle.

6. Breathe out through the mouth as you separate the
hands and bring them out to the sides and down — in
the position you started in. Let your head resume its
forward position at the same time.

7. Repeat this a few times, breathing in through the nose
as you raise the arms in front of you and breathing out
through the mouth as you bring them out and down.
Make the movement soft, gentle and flowing.

The Heart Sutra is the most cited and revered
passage in Mahayana Buddhist tradition. In his
teachings, Buddha extolled the importance of key
qualities of kindness, openness and enlightenment.

AN OPEN HEART

A stylized heart, like two inverted teardrops, is used around the world as a symbol of love and romance. It's a pictorial way of expressing the widespread idea that our emotions, above all affection and romantic attachment, reside in the beating core of the self. But this concept only emerged in the Middle Ages – before then the heart was seen in the West as the repository of memory. Further back, the Ancient Egyptians believed that the heart represented life and honour.

The Heart of Love

A beautiful thirteenth-century French poem, 'Le Roman De La Poire', tells how a maiden peels a pear with her teeth and then hands it to her suitor as a sign of commitment. He is depicted offering up his heart in return. This is thought to be the first illustrative depiction of the notion that we 'give our hearts' to those we love. The heart as offering was central to the Medieval concept of courtly love, in which young men were inspired to acts of bravery in order to 'win the heart' of their beloved. A later French tapestry, entitled *The Gift of the Heart*, again shows the heart being proffered as a sign of love. In this later work the heart no longer resembles a pear, as in the earlier image, but is the symmetrical shape that we recognize today – and a brilliant, passionate red. The idea that love is a gift freely given has become deeply embedded in our culture, as has the idea that to bestow or receive a heart's love is a source of deep and ineffable bliss.

LOVING KINDNESS

There are many types of meditation from Buddhist tradition, but one of the most popular is the loving-kindness meditation. This meditation has been shown to increase self-compassion and love, with far-reaching benefits for emotional healing and reduction of depressive symptoms. The practice of loving kindness involves the repetition of key phrases that have the power to evoke a natural state of helpfulness, gentleness and unconditional love for yourself and toward others.

1. Find a quiet place to sit – a room in your home where you will be undisturbed or a tranquil place outside. Sit comfortably on a chair or cross-legged on a cushion on the floor; the key to meditation is to find your natural comfort level so you may free your mind from your bodily concerns to focus on your meditative process.

2. You are now ready to take four cleansing breaths. Gradually breathe in through the nostrils and exhale through your mouth. On the last cleansing breath speak out loud the phrase: 'May I be well in mind, body and soul'. Keep repeating this breathing technique and saying the phrase over again until you can imagine yourself in your most alive state of being.

3. Next, work in the same way with the phrase: 'May I be helpful, loving and kind'. Again, visualize yourself

being the very phrase you keep repeating. For instance, seeing yourself being loving to a child or a younger version of yourself can reinforce your practice.

4. After a few minutes, still staying with the meditative process, consider changing the phrase to extend to others. While substituting the 'I' for 'you', it might be helpful to think of a specific person that you wish to direct your loving kindness towards. As you picture this person, know that your loving-kindness quotient is growing stronger.

5. Practise this meditation for a few weeks and see yourself become less critical and more heart-full.

THE RIGHT WORDS

Each phrase in the loving kindness meditation begins with the words 'May I be…' – add 'safe', 'well', 'loving', 'open' or something else that will inspire your kind-hearted nature. There is no one perfect phrase, so find the one that works best for you.

DOUBLE THE HAPPINESS

The double happiness symbol is often used in Chinese weddings as a symbol of the couple's joy in coming together, as well as for New Year and other celebrations. It's a great reminder of the part other people play in our happiness, and the role we play in theirs. The 'double compliments' exercise is a way to bring greater positivity to any relationship — from partnerships to friendships to acquaintances. Try to put it into action every day.

1. Give compliments freely. This encourages you to focus on what you like about those you are close to, and it is an easy way to help make others feel happy — research shows that receiving a compliment can activate the same part of the brain as receiving cash — it's really a little gift. Rather than focusing on someone's outward appearance, make your words address a personal achievement, an action, or a character trait that you have noticed. And make sure you mean it — to make someone feel good, a compliment needs to be genuine.

2. Accept compliments gladly. When you receive praise, be aware of any tendency to bat it away, discount it, or explain why you are undeserving of it. Many of us do this, but it can make ourselves and the giver of the compliment feel uncomfortable. So, next time you are complimented, take a deep breath, and allow yourself to believe it. Smile and say thank you!

The double happiness symbol features the Chinese
character for 'joy' repeated twice. It represents love,
happiness and good fortune.

THE POWER OF DANCE

D ance is fantastic exercise for your body – and great for your happiness levels! Ancient philosophers talked of its wonderful effect: Plato claimed that it was the art that 'most influences the soul', and Nietzsche argued that a day when we don't dance is a day lost. Throughout time, dance has been a way to express deep emotions, to lift spirits, to celebrate and to commiserate, and to make social connections. The Native Americans had sacred dances to call for rain in times of drought, as did shamanic dancers in ancient China. Ritual dances are part of religious worship in Tibet, Bali, India and other countries; and in many cultures dance is an age-old way of telling stories that pass down generations.

The Hula

In Hawaii hula dancing is an art form, a spiritual practice and a spectacle that has kept visitors flocking to the islands. There are many different versions of the hula legend, often including the volcano goddess Pele. In one story, Pele's youngest sister Hi'iaka learns the dance from her friend Hōpoe. One day Pele sent Hi'iaka on a quest to bring her lover to her; Hi'iaka agreed on condition that Pele protected her friend. But as the days passed, Pele became impatient. Her rage bubbled up and then cascaded over the land until it covered the beach where Hōpoe stood waiting for her fate. She was transformed into a huge boulder of lava that balanced on the seashore, seeming to dance whenever the waves or the wind moved it. Thereafter she was known as the Dancing Stone of Puna.

GET MOVING

'Dancing is poetry with arms and legs.'
CHARLES BAUDELAIRE

There are plenty of scientific studies that back up our instinctive feeling that dancing makes us feel great. Swedish researchers discovered that teenage girls who danced regularly felt happier about themselves than those who didn't, and an Australian study found that going to tango classes can help reduce levels of anxiety and stress. You don't have to be a world-class performer to benefit — improvising and having fun are what matters most. Try this mini dance-a-thon next time you are feeling low to allow your body to work through your feelings and connect you to greater happiness.

1. Spend a few minutes walking around your home, getting in touch with your body. Swing your arms, breathe deeply, feel the ground beneath your feet. Allow your movements to become more exaggerated in a smooth and fluid way.

2. When you feel ready, put on music with a good melody and a rhythmic beat — as loud as you can. Let yourself go as you dance — seeing where your body takes you.

3. Keep dancing. Don't worry about how 'good' you are and let go of any preconceived notions of what dance should look like. If you want to make circles with your hips or do star jumps — go for it. There are no rules.

4. Spend some time letting your movements emanate from your chest area, then from the hip area. Feel the difference without thinking about it too much.

5. Try going from smooth fluid movements to choppy and staccato ones, large movements to small movements – as the spirit moves you.

6. Allow yourself to stay with a particular movement for as long as feels right – or change from one to another as quickly as you like. Whatever feels right to you is what is right for you.

7. When you feel ready to slow it down, change the music to something more measured – a classical tune perhaps. Let your movements become calmer and slower.

8. Stop when you want to. Maybe walk around your home again or sit down with a glass of water to relax. Enjoy!

TRY A DIFFERENT STYLE

There are many different styles of dance to choose from: lindy hop, ballet, flamenco, Bollywood, to name a few. Or try therapeutic ecstatic dance, which is free-form and specifically developed to allow people to express feelings.

THE MEDICINE OF LAUGHTER

*'Life is worth living as long as
there's a laugh in it.'*

L.M. MONTGOMERY, *ANNE OF GREEN GABLES*

Laughing Buddha is a Chinese deity called Budai or Pu-Tai, who is seen as a reincarnation of the Buddha. He is normally shown carrying prayer beads and a cloth sack containing his few possessions. Rubbing his belly is said to bring good luck, and he is a reminder that joy and abundance comes from within rather than from material success. Be inspired by Budai, and try some 'laughter yoga'. Don't worry if you feel awkward to begin with. Any kind of laughter releases feel-good endorphins, dopamine and serotonin, into the body, creating a sense of well-being and contentment.

1. Stand up and take a few deep breaths. Then start clapping out a simple rhythm with your hands. As you clap, move your hands from side to side and up and down.
2. Now sound out laughing sounds – like 'ha ha ha', 'he he he' – in time with your claps. Keep breathing deeply as you do this.
3. Gradually speed up your clapping and your laughing sounds, moving your whole body as you laugh. Let the sounds turn into a proper belly laugh – you can stop

clapping, or release the idea that the sounds need to synchronize with the claps. Keep laughing for a full minute as you move and sway your body — allow yourself to let go.

———— ∽∾∾⌒⌒⌒ ————

Budai is a good reminder that laughter is an essential part of life: a good belly laugh is a great way to release stress and boost your mood.

———— ∽∾∾⌒ ————

JOYFUL VOICES

M usic, and particularly human song, has long been used as a way of expressing emotions – be that joy and love, or sadness and heartbreak – and has the power of moving both listeners and participants deeply. Joyful singing is part of spiritual worship in cultures across the world and has been throughout the ages. For Aborigines and Hindus, Celts and Israelites, song has always been the language of the heart, an integral part of the way that human beings express themselves and honour their gods.

The Beauty of Song

One Indian tale relates the story of boastful Narada who believed himself to be a virtuoso singer. One day, he came across a group of beings who were twisting in pain on the ground. They were the ragas – the patterns of notes that form Indian classical music – who had taken human form and were now suffering great hurt because of his poor singing. Horrified, Narada called on the gods to help relieve their torment. The god Shiva appeared and sang with such beauty that the ragas were healed. Listening to the wonderful music the god Vishnu was so overcome that he began to melt like ice. Upon seeing this, Shiva collected the drops of water that fell from Vishnu's body, using them to form the maiden Ganga. She in turn became the sacred river Ganges, which purifies everything. This story is a wonderful metaphor for the magical power of music, which uplifts us, flows through the consciousness like running water, and cleanses our minds of stress and melancholy.

SING YOUR HEART OUT

'Sing like no one's listening, love like you've never been hurt, dance
like no one's watching and live like it's heaven on earth.'

MARK TWAIN

It's likely that singing evolved as a way of creating a sense of community, uniting people in joyful harmony and encouraging social cohesion. It is certainly true that singing – whether in a group or alone – boosts feelings of happiness and well-being. It promotes deep aerobic breathing, which is integral to good health, too. Here are six ways to put your body and soul into singing, and maximize the physical and emotional benefits.

Breathe deeply You sing better when you practise abdominal breathing – see page 172 for an exercise to help you do just that. And the reverse is true, too: singing encourages you to breathe better so improves feelings of alertness and well-being.

Open wide If your mouth is partly closed, then the sound can't come out – you create more power with a big mouth! Practise by loudly sounding out the vowel sounds – a e i o u – with an exaggerated mouth position.

Stand tall Having good posture optimizes your breathing and relaxes the body, both of which make your voice sound better. Practise the qigong exercise on page 56 to aid your voice.

Consider classes   If you want to improve your voice invest in some time with a professional coach. A good teacher will show you simple exercises to help loosen the vocal chords and improve your range.

Sing with real feeling   Put your heart into your singing, and resonate with the meaning of the words.

Let go of your inhibitions   Most of all, don't worry about your performance but focus on enjoying the act of singing. If you feel shy, try singing in the shower!

JOIN A GROUP

There are singing groups for all genres of music, from rock to gospel. Joining a choir is a perfect way to lift your spirits; researchers have found that the combination of singing and socializing increases well-being and a sense of belonging.

GOOD VIBES ONLY

'Do not protect yourself by a fence, but rather by your friends.'

CZECH PROVERB

It's a fact that people are happier when they surround themselves with other happy people. Researchers at the University of California and Harvard Medical School confirmed that happiness can pass from one person to another in a chain reaction. But we don't always have total control over who we spend time with — so this exercise shows you how to shield yourself from those who lower your spirits.

1. In the morning — or before you spend time with someone who you know to have a negative effect on you — spend a few minutes breathing deeply. Then close your eyes and imagine that glowing warm light is cascading down from the sky and all over your body.
2. Keep visualizing this cascade of light, imagining it creating an impenetrable boundary through which negativity cannot penetrate.
3. Open your eyes, but maintain this sense of protection. As you go through your day, pause what you are doing from time to time to close your eyes and reconnect with this sensation. When you come into contact with negativity, remind yourself that the glowing light is preventing it from affecting you.

Native Americans traditionally used shields not
only for physical protection but to keep them from
spiritual harm as well. 'Medicine shields', created with
the help of shamans, were attached to their horses
and homes to invoke protection.

CULTIVATE KARMA

When it comes to happiness you reap what you sow, according to the concept of karma, which is a feature of Hinduism and other Eastern religions. Karma is interpreted slightly differently in each tradition, but in Hinduism karma is a law of nature that ensures our lives are governed by a 'system of cause and effect'. Thus, our actions in the past have an effect on us, for good or ill, in the future. Although there's no specific idea of karma that originated in the West, folk tales often warn of both the virtuous and the bad getting their just deserts.

Snow White and Rose Red

In the tale of Snow White and Rose Red, two young girls live with their widowed mother. One winter's evening, a bear arrives at their door and begs to be allowed to warm himself at their fire. Although frightened, the family let him in and he becomes their friend. When summer comes the girls are walking through the forest when they come across a dwarf in difficulty. They rescue him, but instead of being grateful he berates them. This happens repeatedly – until one day they find him about to be eaten by the bear. The dwarf screams at the bear to attack the girls instead – but the bear, recognizing the girls as his friends, kills the dwarf and instantly transforms into a handsome prince. The two girls marry the prince and his brother, and all live happily ever after. The moral is that goodness is always be rewarded – even if the recipient is ungrateful or downright evil!

LITTLE ACTS OF KINDNESS

'A single act of kindness throws out roots in all directions,
and the roots spring up and make new trees.'

AMELIA EARHART

Whether you believe in karma or not, it's a fact that doing good deeds can boost your happiness levels. A study conducted by the University of Columbia asked a group of people to do at least six acts of kindness a week – and found that not only did their mood improve but they also became more satisfied with their relationships. Other research suggests that kindness is contagious: people on the receiving end of a kind act are more likely to help others. So one small favour can create a domino effect. Bring a little kindness therapy into your week with these simple ideas:

Hold the door open for people – a simple gesture but one that will be appreciated.

Let someone go before you in the queue for the supermarket, at a coffee shop or getting on the bus.

Give up your seat on public transport to allow others to sit down.

Buy the coffees when you meet a friend, bring a coffee back for a colleague who is working through lunch, or pay for the stranger behind you in a queue.

TAKE NOTE

A nice way to bring more kindness into your life is
to keep a 'Good Deeds' diary. Record one act of
kindness in your journal each evening. Not only will
the act of noting these small gestures make you feel
happy about yourself, but it will also encourage you
to go on and do more!

Pick up some litter in the street — a cleaner neighbourhood makes
everyone feel brighter and is kind to the environment as well.

Practise road love rather than rage: let a driver into your lane, or
wave them into that parking space you had your eye on.

Do a chore that you know your partner or a family member hates.

Buy flowers for teachers at a local school, or for nurses or
receptionists at your local hospital.

Chat to an elderly neighbour and ask if they need help with their
weekly shopping.

SMILE FOR HAPPINESS

If you want to feel happier, smile more! That's the conclusion of many scientific studies that have found that the very act of smiling — even when it is forced — activates the pleasure and reward areas of the brain and releases endorphins into the body, making us feel happier. What is more, it seems that we are hard-wired to return a smile when we see one; so when you smile at other people, the chances are that they will smile right back, creating a ripple effect. Take these little opportunities to smile more every day:

Start your day sunny   As soon as you wake up, take a deep breath in and out and smile.

Hey good looking   When you look in the mirror to straighten your hair or clean your teeth, smile at yourself. Make it a really big grin. Try wishing yourself a good morning too.

Happy talk   Answer a phone call smiling: it has an effect on your voice and will radiate positivity down the line.

In the detail   Make eye contact and smile at waiters or shop assistants — smiling makes any interaction more pleasurable. Always smile when you greet someone or take your leave.

Make an entrance   Smile when you enter a room, even if nobody else is there!

FAKE IT TO MAKE IT

If you really feel you have nothing to smile about,
put a pencil in between your lips. This places the
face in a similar position to a smile and can have
the same mood-boosting effect it might even
prompt a genuine grin!

CROWNING GLORY

'With laurel crowned as conqueror, there he lived in joy and honour.'

GEOFFREY CHAUCER

The laurel wreath was a crown of honour and symbol of achievement for the ancient Greeks, and its association with success has continued through the ages. Napoleon I chose the laurel wreath as an emblem of his Empire, emulating Julius Caesar before him who wore a laurel crown. In modern times, a laurel wreath has been depicted on the gold medals given to winners of the Olympics. The foliage also has an association with achievement in learning – Italian students are called *laureato* when they graduate and wear a crown of laurel; and in the UK the title of Poet Laureate is bestowed on an outstanding poet who is charged with writing works to mark important moments in the life of the nation.

The Immortal Laurel

In Greek myth, the mischievous Eros, god of love, used his powers to play a trick on Apollo, with whom he had a quarrel. Eros fired two of his arrows: one at Apollo to make him fall in love with the beautiful river nymph Daphne, and one at Daphne to make her view Apollo with revulsion. Crazed with desire, Apollo pursued Daphne, but she was determined to get away from him – and in her desperation she called on the river god to save her. The river god transformed her into a laurel tree to put her beyond Apollo's reach. Seeing the object of his desire so transformed, Apollo used his power to make the laurel immortal: he turned her leaves evergreen and deemed the tree to be sacred. This is why in Greece laurel crowns were awarded to the winners of the Pythian games, held in Apollo's honour.

CELEBRATE SUCCESS

Today people find many reasons to celebrate special occasions, but what about celebrating ourselves? According to *Psychology Today*, being acknowledged for what we accomplish can translate into more self-confidence. Recognizing our successes — both big and small — can also help us to make better choices, advance ourselves and, in the long run, find more contentment in life. So why not dispense with the criticism and start recognizing your achievements, wearing your proverbial laurel wreath proudly? Here are some tips to get yourself into an achieving state of mind:

Spruce up   It may seem superficial, but taking pride in our physical appearance can be a powerful confidence-booster. Adding a new scarf or trying a different nail colour can foster a more positive attitude. If it's too hard to find the energy to dress up, start small by improving your personal hygiene and general health. The more you take care of yourself, the more success you'll find in any little task you complete.

Do what you love   One simple way to motivate ourselves to further success is to find examples from our own lives of what has, or is, going well. There is always something to point to that can stimulate you to aim higher and try harder. Inspiring yourself with what you love and enjoy — in the past or present — can lead to feelings of emotional satisfaction and achievement.

Cultivate a new perspective You don't have to do epic things to feel a sense of achievement. The potential for success is in every little step we take towards our goals, whether that is in career, home, education or relationships. Every time you do something, no matter the scale, focus on what you did accomplish, instead of what still needs to get done.

Promote yourself Talk yourself up with words of affirmation such as 'I can make that happen', or 'I'll succeed at that'. Tell yourself that you'll be triumphant no matter what. Believing in your success will boost your confidence and inner contentment. Visualising meeting your goals and celebrating your accomplishments can also help you on the path to success.

Hand yourself success Set realistic goals and see your motivation get recharged. Celebrating each step along the way will reinforce a positive attitude and make your achievement more momentous.

Say it out loud Talk about your success to others to keep your spirits high and inspire others to achieve their goals, too. Achievement gives your happy neurotransmitters (such as dopamine) and endorphins a big bump. Celebrating a win on social media or simply with your close friends also lets others know that positive change is possible for them too.

HEALING THE CRACKS

'The wound is the place where the light enters you'.

RUMI

We can often create unhappiness by judging ourselves and others too harshly. The Japanese art of repair — *kintsukuroi* — is a useful reminder that our history, sufferings and mistakes are part of what makes us who we are, and we are all the more interesting for our imperfections. This exercise helps us to embrace our failings and stay positive.

See the positive   If there is a painful event that has changed you, try to acknowledge any useful lessons that you have learned. A regret over our actions can be a turning point, a moment when we resolve to live life differently, to become more adventurous or more compassionate.

Make amends   If you are feeling regretful about your own actions then consider whether there is something you can do to make amends. Often, acknowledging mistakes and owning responsibilities can heal the cracks.

Be present   The past is the past and cannot be undone. But we can use our mistakes to shape our present actions — and our futures.

Stay open Accidents or mishaps may look like a disaster, but often a situation can be salvaged or our energies can be redirected — if only we can stay open to the opportunities that come our way.

In *kintsukuroi* a broken pot is repaired with gold in a way that draws attention to the mend and celebrates the idea that the damage makes the object unique and all the more exquisite.

GET COSY

The Danes are perhaps the happiest nation in the world, regularly ranking top in the UN World Happiness Report. What is their secret? It may have something to do with *hygge*, an untranslatable Danish word that denotes a kind of cosy contentment. Here's how to introduce more of this wonderful way of being into your life – especially during the cold months.

Up the snug factor In winter it is dark sixteen hours a day in Denmark, so the Danes have perfected the art of making their homes feel inviting. Think sensual: soft throws and cushions, ambient lighting with lamps or fairy lights, a blazing hearth... anything that makes it feel like your house is giving you a hug.

Think simplicity *Hygge* is never complicated! Declutter your space and go for neutral colours that are easy on the eye.

Embrace the small things *Hygge* is about enjoying life's small indulgences – eating Scandinavian cinnamon buns, wearing warm bed socks, reading the weekend papers, making real coffee and appreciating every sip...

Prioritize togetherness The Danes are big on spending time with family and friends. Find a meaningful activity to bring a group together – invite people round and cook together, play board games or enjoy crafts such as card-making or knitting.

SHINE A LIGHT

'How far that little candle throws its beams.
So shines a good deed in a naughty world'.

WILLIAM SHAKESPEARE

T he flickering light of a flame must have been a comforting sight to our ancestors. A candle can represent hope in times of darkness, and also the kind of spiritual illumination that can give life meaning and a sense of inner joy. Candles feature in many religions for this reason: Hindus, Christians, Jews and Buddhists – members of other faiths too – light candles as an act of worship. At the Russian Orthodox celebration of Easter – the highlight of the calendar – everyone holds a candle that is lit from the nearest person, symbolizing the fact that the light of faith can be shared without diminishing the original source.

A Symbol of Constancy and Hope

In *Doctor Zhivago*, his epic novel of Russia, Boris Pasternak uses a single candle as an image of hope and love. The heroine Lara sits by a window on a freezing night, with a single candle for illumination that melts a hole in the ice on the window. Zhivago – who has yet to meet her – drives past below and notices this sole point of light. He remembers this moment forever, though he never knows that in that instant he was connected to Lara, the future love of his life. That moment is also described obliquely in 'Winter's Night', one of the cycle of poems by Zhivago that form the last chapter of the novel. In the poem the tiny flame continues to burn despite the raging blizzards that blow – like a small hope that survives when everything militates against it.

FLAME MEDITATION

'All the darkness in the world cannot extinguish the light of a single candle.'

ST FRANCIS OF ASSISI

Meditation, which is known to increase feelings of happiness and well-being, often involves concentrating your attention on a single point of focus, which might be the breath or a physical object that you can gaze at. In Hinduism, this form of meditation is called *trataka* and is most often done using a flame. The exercise can bring about a sense of stillness and calm that allows you to let go of day-to-day concerns. It is deeply relaxing and a great way to reset your mind when you are feeling overwhelmed.

1. Get your space ready. Draw the curtains or close the blinds and dim the lights. Place your candle in a safe place where it will be level with or just below your eye level and light it.
2. Settle into a comfortable sitting position, one that you can hold for a few minutes without having to move. Breathe deeply and naturally.
3. Now gaze at the candle flame. Keep your gaze soft but focused — you are not staring hard but nor should you be glazing over. Your eyes may water a little.
4. Keep all of your attention on the flame as you breathe in and out, letting your breath find its natural rhythm.

SWEET SCENT

Choose a natural candle for a warming subtle
scent: beeswax or soya candles work well. You
could also use an aromatherapy candle with an
essential oil – rosemary, lemon or cyprus oil are
all good for encouraging focus.

5. When you need to rest your eyes, close them and keep
   your focus on the imprint of the flame that appears.
   Then, when it starts to fade, open your eyes and gaze at
   the candle flame again.
6. You may notice that your peripheral vision starts to fade
   and you become more and more focused on the flame.
7. If thoughts start to intrude on your experience, notice
   they are there and redirect your focus back to the flame.
8. When you are ready to end the meditation, blow out the
   candle. Spend a minute or two slowly broadening your
   awareness to encompass your surroundings.

WALK IT OUT

Across cultures and times, people have gone on pilgrimages to find spiritual peace — Muslims have the hajj, Catholics may walk El Camino de Santiago in Spain, and Anglican pilgrims head to Canterbury. Walking is a way of uniting body and mind and naturally boosting mood — but you don't have to have a destination to benefit: this walking meditation can be done in a hallway.

1. You'll need an area that is about 10 metres long — a hallway or a quiet outdoor space — for this exercise.
2. Stand for a moment and take a deep breath, relaxing the body as you exhale. Bring your attention to the soles of the feet, focusing on the contact with the ground.
3. Then, very slowly step one foot forwards: notice how the heel lifts first then the ball of the foot before it moves. As you place the heel on the floor in front of you before rolling the rest of the foot down, notice how the back foot starts to lift in readiness for the next step.
4. Continue stepping, focusing all your awareness on what you can feel in the foot. When you reach the end of your 10-metre area, pause for a moment. Turn with the same awareness, then walk back the same way.
5. If you notice you mind wandering, bring your attention gently back. Resist any sense of wanting to hurry and simply focus on the act of walking for this short period.

TAKE A DIP

'A bath refreshes the body, tea refreshes the mind.'

JAPANESE SAYING

The Turkish have *hammans*, Russians go to the *banya*, the Japanese to *onsen*, Koreans to *jjimjilbangs* and Native Americans have sweat lodges. The tradition of communal bathhouses crosses continents and aeons. There's evidence that nomadic tribes would soak in natural hot springs together in Neolithic times, and in the Indus Valley, in modern-day Pakistan, archeologists excavated a large pool dubbed the 'Great Bath' which was built in around 2,500 BC.

A World of Bathing

Any visitor to Korea will head for a *jjimjilbang*, where you can have a scrub-down from an *ajumma* (auntie), then soak in a communal pool and enjoy healing spa treatments. It's an age-old tradition that began, according to one story, when a hunter's arrow pierced the skin of a deer but didn't kill it. The hunter followed the wounded deer's trail and found him near the hot spring called Baegam Oncheon. Noticing that the deer's injuries had been magically healed, the hunter himself took a dip in the magical water. Koreans today often visit the *jjimjilbang* weekly. It is a social occasion that people enjoy with friends and family — and this is true of bathhouses all around the world, enjoyed as social places as well as places of healing, calm and self-nurture. While we may not all have access to a weekly spa trip, we can aim to build some relaxation time into our schedules to unwind in a soothing bath.

CLEANSE THE SOUL

Today we bathe not just to wipe away the dirt of the day, but to engage in full relaxation, detoxification of the mind and body, and for emotional rejuvenation. Mindful bathing is an undistracted, luxurious practice of experiencing your emotions and physicality at the same time. Here are some simple steps to create your own bathing ritual:

1. Find a time to bathe that works for you. Ending the day with a bath is a great way to encourage sleepiness, while starting the day with a bath can help you calm your disposition.

2. Decide on what you will put in your bath. Using herbs, essential oils, floral petals or bath salts offer sensations and aromas that intensify your bathing experience. They also add a wonderful element to your bath time as you allow your body to steep in its quenching and healing powers.

3. Turn your attention to the space around your tub. Try turning off the lights and adding some candles around the basin or on the shelves – a lovely way of illuminating your space. Consider burning some incense to add pleasant aromas: scents of lavender, sage or sandalwood help to enliven your senses. Soft music can quiet thoughts and ease tensions.

4. Run the water at a nice warm temperature. As you watch the water pour into your tub try to think about washing away the worries of the day or the day before. As you observe the water rise, see your level of consciousness rise along with it. Use your hands to slowly stir in the salts, oils or bubble bath, and think about how you can be aware of what is around you and still be yourself.

5. Disrobe and take a moment to appreciate your body, without judgement or criticism. As you step into your bath, allow your body to gently melt into the water and soak up all the water's refreshment. Breathe deeply, inhaling all the wonderful smells that surround you through your nostrils, then slowly exhale.

6. As you begin to wash your body draw your attention to each body part. See how soap bubbles rise, fall and are washed away in an instant. Our troubles are like bubbles — most of them seem so big yet can vanish into nothingness.

7. Fully indulge in this delightful cleanse. Observe yourself luxuriating and relaxing. Take in all the sounds, smells and the feel of the water enveloping your body. As you step out of the tub, let your towel embrace you, as if to say thank you. Your moment of gratitude urges you to make this special mindful ritual a frequent practice.

NOTHING IS PERMANENT

'All things must pass'.

THE BUDDHA

When we embrace the Buddhist idea that all things pass and nothing stays the same forever, we gain greater inner peace. This is because when times are difficult we know they will not last forever, meaning that we can bear them more easily. Equally, when times are good, we know they too will not last, so it is pointless to try to cling on to them. Here are three ways to put the Buddha's philosophy into practice and maintain your inner contentment:

Let it wash over   In times of stress or anxiety, imagine a difficult feeling as a wave – it arises, builds to a crest and then subsides. Sometimes you just need to surf the wave.

Stand strong   When you feel overwhelmed, visualize yourself as a mountain – difficulties may buffet your surface like the wind, but they do not erode the essential strength at your core.

Positive affirmation   Use the phrase 'this too shall pass' as a mantra. You may like to sit quietly and repeat this to yourself, or use it as a comforting phrase during difficult periods.

The Buddha taught that peace comes
from within, not from our external
circumstances. And one of his key lessons
was the observation that all things pass
in time. Remembering this can help us to
weather painful times and foster an inner
contentment that stays with us whatever is
happening in our lives.

CHAPTER THREE:
MYTHOLOGY & FOLKLORE

'Hansel took his little sister by the hand, and
followed the pebbles which shone like newly–
coined silver pieces, and showed them the way.'

JACOB AND WILHELM GRIMM, GRIMM'S FAIRY TALES

CELEBRATE NEW STARTS

The first day of spring, 20 March has been designated International Happiness Day. The choice of the spring equinox – the day when the hours of daylight begin at last to exceed the hours of night – is no accident. In the southern hemisphere this switch occurs in September, but wherever you are in the world, there are many joyous celebrations associated with the start of spring and its themes of new life. The Hopi tribe in North America have a myth that explains the coming spring through the tale of the Blue Corn Maiden. It is surprisingly similar to the Greek story of Persephone and Hades, god of the underworld.

The Blue Corn Maiden

Of all the corn maiden sisters, who bring the gift of food to the world, the Blue Corn Maiden was the most beautiful. One day the spirit of the cold months, Winter Katsina, caught sight of her and immediately fell in love. He took her to his home and imprisoned her there. One day, Katsina left the Blue Corn Maiden alone and she managed to escape. Finding some yucca leaves, she used these to make a fire that melted the snow and allowed the spirit of the warm months, Summer Katsina, through. Rather than fight, he and Winter Katsina came to an agreement: the Blue Corn Maiden would spend half the year with Winter Katsina, when the corn would not grow, and the rest with Summer Katsina. Springtime is the start of her stay with Summer Katsina, and any late flurries of snow are Winter Katsina's rages when she leaves him.

NEW GROWTH

'Spring is the time of plans and projects.'
LEO TOLSTOY

Most people are naturally happier in spring. It is lighter, which helps us feel more alert and also boosts levels of the feel-good neurotransmitter serotonin, and the weather is warmer, so we are more likely to spend time outdoors and be more active — both of which help with the release of mood-enhancing endorphins. Here are some ways to make the most of spring:

Inspire inner growth Since spring is a time of green shoots and new buds, it is also the season when our thoughts naturally turn to our personal growth. Mark out some time to think about what areas of yourself and your life you want to grow or revitalize this year. Set some goals for yourself — see the exercise on page 112 for some help with this.

Use that energy You may notice that you feel more energetic and vibrant at this time of year. If you practise yoga or meditation or have an exercise regime, this is a great time to bring extra discipline and routine to it. If you do not exercise regularly, this could be the perfect time to get started — exercise is proven to be a good antidote to stress and to have a positive effect on mood and well-being.

Enjoy new life Get outdoors and walk among the bluebells or other spring flowers: be inspired by the flourishing life you see all around you. Bring plants and flowers into your home to add colour and life to every room.

Go bright Change your wardrobe from dull blacks and greys to more colourful and lighter clothes. You'll feel an instant boost of confidence if you wear red or orange.

Have a traditional spring clean Cleaning your home from top to bottom gives you a psychological boost. Many spring festivals are preceded by a major clean-up, not only to freshen the home but also as a way of sweeping out the past and removing any evil spirits. The Persian spring festival of Nowruz is traditionally preceded by a ritual called *khaneh tekani*, or 'shaking the house', when everything from carpets to silverware gets a good clean.

FIND YOUR FLOW

The muses of Ancient Greece represented key areas of creative life, and various female deities across cultures have been associated with handicrafts. Crafting — whether knitting, jam-making, baking, sewing or weaving — can boost your mental well-being. That's the conclusion of a numerous studies, including research conducted in New Zealand which found that doing crafts one day led to greater 'flourishing' the next (flourishing is a term used to encompass both happiness and meaning). Here are some simple ideas to inspire creativity:

Try something new Mastering a new craft can give you a deep sense of satisfaction. Learn from a book, take a class or watch YouTube videos. Set yourself small achievable targets and enjoy the process of meeting them.

Go for flow Psychologists say that we get the most satisfaction from engaging in a 'flow' activity, which is a task that we can become completely absorbed in, has a clear goal, and provides us with an instant sense of feedback. In pottery, for example, we can immerse ourselves in the act of moulding the clay, we have the clear goal of creating a pot, and we can see how it is taking shape.

Create the time Rather than assuming you will fit your crafting in whenever everything else is done, schedule in a chunk of time when you can concentrate on it.

The deities associated with spinning, weaving and many other crafts are female, including the Norse goddess Frigg, who was said to work on a jewelled spinning wheel. Scandinavians once called the constellation of Orion by the name *Friggerock*, 'Frigga's distaff' – which is a stick used for winding thread.

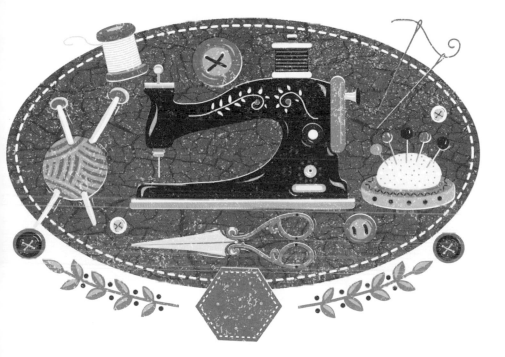

DON'T GIVE UP

I t is a fact that we cannot expect to be happy all the time, and throughout our lives we will face difficulties. Many myths deal with struggle, telling the tale of a hero or heroine who faces seemingly overwhelming odds but ultimately overcomes them. Often success comes because the hero does not give up; no matter what life or the gods throw at them, they always keep their goal in mind and their focus clear.

Jason and the Golden Fleece

In this story from Greek mythology, Jason is challenged to fetch the sacred golden fleece, owned by King Aeëtes and guarded by the Hydra, a fearsome many-headed dragon. Completing this task will enable him to regain the throne his uncle has denied him. Jason and a band of heroic comrades, the Argonauts, sail off on their quest and face many perils along the way. When they finally arrive at their destination, Jason is set a new trial that he seems doomed to fail: to plough a field using fire-breathing oxen and sow it with the teeth of dragons. The dragon's teeth sprout and grow into an army of warriors that oppose Jason and his crew. With the magical help of Aeëtes' daughter, Medea, Jason defeats the warriors and steals the fleece from under the Hydra's nose. Fleeing from Aeëtes' wrath with Medea, Jason encounters still more dangers. But his determination never wavers, and he never ceases to believe he can achieve his goal. Sure enough, eventually Jason reaches home, with the reward of the fleece and with Medea at his side.

SET A GOAL

How often do you ask yourself if you are headed in the direction of your passion? It is so easy to get sidetracked and leave your aims and ambitions behind. It takes real commitment to reach a goal. Use the exercise below when you feel that you have lost your drive and ambition, as a guide to setting clear, achievable goals.

1. Make the positive decision that now is the time to make a meaningful change in your life, such as getting fit, finding a new career or returning to school.
2. Before committing, check in with yourself that this is the best time to take on this challenge. Look at what you have going on in your life in terms of financial, emotional and mental health. If you are already spread too thin, consider if this goal is something that you can truly take on right now.
3. Explore your priorities – goals which line up with your values are more likely to be achieved.
4. Next try imagining yourself in the future doing the very thing you desire. Do you like what you see? Does it inspire you to meet this goal head on and challenge yourself now?

5. Consider discussing your goal with someone; this could be a partner, friend, or family member. Sharing your goal can help you be more accountable.

6. Now you are ready to make a realistic plan towards your goal. Establishing clear, measurable steps will help keep you motivated. For instance, if you want to return to education, a first step toward that vision might be to enrol in a class by a certain date, or even browsing a course syllabus after work.

7. Lastly, what kind of routine or habits do you need to acquire to make this happen? This is where the real work begins, but it doesn't have to be hard. If you desire weight loss, stopping at fast-food restaurants on the way home from work will need to be replaced with new habits, such as eating an apple you packed or taking a yoga class. This new routine doesn't happen overnight but rather with steady perseverance.

SMALL STEPS

Sustainable change starts with setting realistic, measurable mini-goals and developing new habits that keep moving you ahead. Remember that it's the tiny, consistent steps that help bring about the biggest change.

WELCOME HOME

'Hope smiles from the threshold of the year to come,
whispering, "it will be happier".'

ALFRED LORD TENNYSON

T hresholds — even everyday doorways into houses — are held sacred in many cultures. Throughout time, peoples have adorned the entrances of their homes with shields, lucky charms and spiritual icons, all intended to promote the happiness and protection of the family within. And all of us can benefit from a threshold ritual that marks the transition between home life and working life. This is a way of leaving any stress outside and embracing the warmth and calm of our personal space. Try doing these three things every time you arrive home:

1. Take a moment to pause at your front door and breathe deeply — allow yourself to arrive. You may like to place a small symbol on or near your front door, to remind you to do this.

2. Make the act of unlocking your door one you perform with full awareness. It's a small deed, but you can use it to bring yourself back into the moment.

3. Remove your shoes when you enter. This is both a practical measure and a psychological one: it reminds you that you are leaving the public space and entering the private one.

In the Hindu pantheon, Ganesha, the elephant-headed
deity, is lord of the threshold and his image is often
displayed at entranceways. In feng shui, a pair of elephants
are considered a fortunate symbol to place at a threshold,
with their trunks raised as if about to shower
the spot with blessings.

THE HEART OF THE HOME

According to Slavic folklore, a benevolent house-goblin called a 'domovoy' can be found living in homes behind the stovepipe or under the floor. The domovoy was thought to be a mischievous but generally benign creature who protected the home, the family and domestic animals. Many families would leave food out for the domovoy, who would do his work at night; and in some parts of Russia, when moving home, peasants would take a burning coal from their old stove and transfer it to the new one as an invitation for the domovoy to come along. We may no longer believe in such supernatural creatures, but the domovoy's concerns remain essential for happiness: a roof over your head, a support network of loved ones and food on the table. Here are some ways to be bring domovoy spirit into the home:

Keep it warm No home, however well appointed, is comfortable when it is chilly, and being cold impacts on your well-being and health. Make sure you are warm when you are at home — thick curtains and draft excluders help in the cold months; wear extra layers as well as heating the home properly.

Tidy up Keep clutter to a minimum — mess creates stress. If your home needs tidying, do it before you go out so that you come back to a welcoming space. Making your bed in the morning is a good discipline to get into, as is clearing away breakfast before you leave in the morning and the dinner things before you go to bed.

Stock the larder   A domovoy would always like there to be a pot of stew bubbling away. The modern equivalent is to make sure you keep the makings of a simple meal in the storecupboard — tins of soup, pasta and sauce and the like. It's hard to be happy when you are hungry!

Have a pet!   Nothing makes a home feel more welcoming than the loving presence of a pet. And research shows that spending time with an animal increases feeling of happiness. A cat on your lap or a dog by your feet is a heartening presence.

THE POWER OF SOLITUDE

Retreat for spiritual contemplation is a feature of many cultures and religions, and it is an essential stage on the journey towards happiness. When you are entirely alone, you cannot help but look inwards and investigate who you truly are. The self-knowledge and ultimate sense of acceptance that can come from this kind of introspection is one of the key elements of genuine contentment. Try these ways of embracing the power of solitude in your life:

1. If your reaction to being alone is an instant need to find someone to talk to or to seek out something to distract you from your thoughts, then try to recognize what you associate with being alone. Many of us conflate solitude with loneliness — but they are not the same at all. Times of solitude should be positive interludes when we recharge and replenish our minds and our bodies. If we can embrace our discomfort around being alone, then we give ourselves opportunity to learn more about ourselves and what makes us truly happy.

2. Set aside half an hour each day when you can be quiet and alone. During this time, do not speak or engage with words (even by reading). Instead, meditate, occupy your mind with something creative, or walk somewhere peaceful. Make sure that your phone is silenced (and ideally out of sight) and switch off all electronic devices.

3. When you are comfortable with a short period of solitude, gift yourself a half or full day of silence once a month. Make this time that you spend entirely by yourself. You can combine this with a day of simplicity (see page 154) if you like, or plan quiet activities that you know you will enjoy.

STANDING TALL

T rees have been a source of wonder for humankind since prehistoric times. Our ancestors had an instinctive understanding that these great works of nature were essential to human existence and honoured them as such. On a practical level trees provide shelter, shade, lumber and sustenance in the form of fruit and nuts. But more than that, trees have always been a metaphor for life and for hope. Their annual cycle, the sprouting and shedding of leaves, is a perfect picture of the universal cycle of life and death, of demise and regeneration. So it is not surprising that trees crop up frequently in mythology – often as the point at which life began.

Tree of the World

The idea of a world tree – with its roots in the underworld, its trunk in the earthly world and its uppermost branches in the heavens – recurs in cultures as diverse as the Mayans and the ancient Latvians. In the Latvian myth, the tree is the beautifully named 'tree of dawn' and has roots of copper, a trunk of gold and leaves of silver. The invocation of these shining metals, and the fact that its name is connected to the daybreak, suggest that the tree was part of a cult of the sun.

FEEL GROUNDED

Many mind-body practices use the image of the tree to promote well-being and inner calm. In yoga, tree pose is a balancing and grounding asana (position). It's a great exercise to do when you are in a flurry of emotion or stress, because it brings you to a point of stillness and focus. Stand tall and broad, breathe deeply and allow yourself to feel good.

1. Stand with both feet on the floor, hip-width apart and toes pointing forwards, and your arms by your side. Spend a few moments relaxing into a stable upright posture, lifting your head so that your neck is in line with your spine, and then slightly dropping the chin so that it is parallel with the floor. Take a few deep, slow breaths into the belly.

2. Now slowly move your weight onto the left foot, letting the right knee bend slowly to facilitate this. Look at a point on the floor or wall a metre or so in front of you — having a stable point of vision will help you to balance.

3. Keep bending the right knee and slowly lift the foot off the floor. Let the knee turn outward as you lift.

4. Rest the sole of the right foot against the inside of your left leg. If you feel wobbly, rest it against the calf (not on the knee) or rest the tips of your toes on the floor with your heel against the opposite ankle. If you feel steady, reach down with your right hand, gently grasp

the ankle of the lifted leg, and place the foot as high up the thigh as is comfortable. Have your right knee pointing outward, so that the lower part of the lifted leg makes a right angle with the supporting leg — again this is an ideal; go with what feels right for your body.

5. If possible, move the right knee back so that your hips are level. Have your hands on your hips, or bring them into a prayer position in front of your chest. Maintain a soft gaze focused on your vision point and breathe deeply throughout.

6. Keep your spine elongated and upright. If you wobble, use your right hand to bring your foot back to position and keep breathing. Pressing the foot into the thigh helps you maintain your balance.

7. Slowly bring the hands down, release the right leg and place the foot back on the floor. Take a breath or two here, and then repeat on the other side.

MINI TREE POSE

If you have any balance issues, try resting your hand on a chair or counter for support. Lift your heel a short distance from the ground, putting as little weight as possible on the ball of the foot. Done regularly (and on both sides) this will build your ability to balance.

MAKE A WISH

The Celts saw natural springs and wells as gifts of the gods. They marked such water sources with statues, or enclosed them in brick or stone and made offerings there. The modern custom of throwing a coin into a pool or fountain is a relic of that practice, but coin-throwing is itself quite ancient: when Coventina's Well in Northumberland was excavated, thousands of Roman coins were found in it. We cannot, of course, wish things into reality. But the act of clarifying what we want can help us act in ways that make our wished-for outcomes more likely. Try the 'best possible self' exercise and see what happens.

1. Set aside time to reflect on what you truly want in life. Imagine yourself six months, one year, or five years down the line, being your best possible self, enjoying your best possible life. Sketch in as many details as you can, making sure that this is a life that appeals to you and is realistic.

2. Now focus in on the character strengths that have helped you to become your best possible self — the determination you have showed to get where you are, the courage you have called on to face challenges, perhaps the open-heartedness you have cultivated in order to develop a happy relationship.

When we throw a coin into a well or
fountain, we are echoing an ancient custom –
and secretly hoping our wish will be granted,
just as our ancestors did.

3. When you feel ready, write down this vision, again
   with as much detail as possible. Include the character
   strengths that are an integral part of your dream.
4. Do this every day for two weeks. It can help you to
   strengthen the aspects of your character that could
   help facilitate the best possible life and it will keep you
   optimistic about the future.

COUNT YOUR BLESSINGS

The cornucopia, or 'horn of plenty', is a symbol of abundance, in particular of the earth's bounty. In modern-day America, a horn-shaped basket is often a centrepiece at the Thanksgiving feast, which is in part a celebration of the gathering-in of the harvest. The cornucopia is related to Medieval tales of a cauldron or cooking pot that never became empty no matter how much food was ladled out of it.

The Horn of Plenty

In a Greek version of the cornucopia myth, the bounteous horn belonged to the goat Amalthaea, the foster mother of baby Zeus who cared for and suckled him when he was in hiding from his murderous father. The child Zeus was blessed with supernatural strength and accidentally wrenched the horn from Amalthaea's head. Her horn then became a new source of nourishment for the god-child, filled with fruit and flowers. In another version of the tale, Hercules, son of Zeus, falls in love with the maiden Deianeira, who is also desired by the river god Achelous. The rivals engage in a battle of strength and Achelous attempts to outwit Hercules by turning himself into first a serpent and then a great bull whereupon the mighty Hercules breaks off one of his horns. Achelous is defeated and nymphs fill the horn with an unending supply of flowers and fruits to celebrate the marriage of Hercules and Deianeira. You'll find the cornucopia in many classical paintings, associated with a variety of other gods and goddess, but always as a source of joyful abundance.

PRACTISE GRATITUDE

'When you realize there is nothing lacking,
the whole world belongs to you'.

LAO TZU

Cornucopia today inspires us to think about what we have and to show gratitude. Being grateful, and expressing gratefulness, helps to keep our brain healthy and our attitude upbeat. Being grateful is not only a state of mind but a lifestyle choice. It has been shown to improve our relationships and overall life satisfaction. Those that study mindfulness point out that we are more likely to stay in the moment when we adopt an attitude of gratitude, and so it counteracts our tendency to procrastinate or worry. Here are some ways you can become more grateful:

Keep a gratitude journal Just writing down what you are grateful for can be an emotional and mental game changer. A journal will help you keep track of your moods, tolerance levels and measure your positivity. By the end of one month you should see yourself more considerate, grateful and optimistic.

Consider everyday items While putting away groceries, ask yourself how many people made it possible for you to buy and take home this food? More specifically, who planted, harvested, transported, packaged and shelved the food you just bought? Reflecting on how everyday things come to us can bump up your gratitude.

Reach out to someone who has been there for you   This could be a text, call, email or written note. Think of a close friend, coach, teacher or parent who has helped make your life's journey better and safer. Even writing cards to those who are no longer with you, but who made a huge difference in your life, can be a lovely act of remembrance and a good way to practise gratitude.

Take a gratitude walk   Step outside and take mental note of all the wonderful natural things that surround you. Try to make a point of nodding thanks to the daily things we take for granted like fresh air, lovely flora, rainwater, trees and the song of the birds above.

Go green   Thank our precious planet in a tangible way by recycling plastics and aluminium or using less paper products, water or heat. By doing your part each day, you will help to raise your gratitude for the world we live in.

Thank someone who makes your life go smoothly   This could be a babysitter, housekeeper or neighbour who looks after your cats when you are away. Whoever it is, let them know how much you appreciate them. Saying thanks is the simplest and kindest form of gratitude known to man.

RISE AGAIN

The Greek and Egyptian myth of the phoenix contains the message that we can arise undefeated from the ashes of despair and failure. In the traditional story the phoenix does not die but is consumed by flames when it grows old, and is then reborn from the embers of its own funeral pyre. The phoenix has equivalents in many other cultures. In Russia it is *zhar-ptitsa*, the 'firebird'; in China the *feng-huang* is also called the 'august rooster'; in Japan there is the *hou-ou*, which manifests itself to mark the beginning of a new era, and so — like the phoenix of Egypt and Greece — is associated with resurgence and new beginnings.

Bird of the Sun

In Ancient Egypt the phoenix had a name, 'Bennu', which seems to mean both 'rise' and 'shine'. It is no surprise then that Bennu was sacred to the people of Heliopolis, the 'city of the sun'. According to one legend, Bennu created itself from the flames of a burning tree and was the first living thing to appear. Its call signalled the start of the world and would be heard again at the world's end. The Greek historian Herodotus treated the Egyptian story as factual, while admitting that he had not seen the bird himself. According to Herodotus, the phoenix appears once in 500 years, has red-and-gold plumage and is the size and shape of an eagle. There is no self-combustion and rising from the ashes in his tale — but he does say that a new phoenix always replaces one that has died, so the essence of the idea of regeneration remains.

NEW BEGINNINGS

'The phoenix hope, can wing her way through desert skies,
and still defying fortune spite; revive from ashes and rise.'

MIGUEL DE CERVANTES

Renewal is an important part of our well-being. Sometimes we have to ditch what's outdated – old clothes, old attitudes, old hurts – if we want to remake ourselves and move on. Traditionally, we make resolutions for change at the start of a new year, but we can embrace new beginnings at any time we choose. If you decide to make a change to help you feel happier and healthier, here are some tips to help you stick to it.

Let something go Just as the phoenix sacrifices itself to make way for its successor, you may have to let something go when you want to embrace a new habit. It may be that you have to stop hitting the snooze button if you want to make time for a healthy breakfast, that you have to let go of an evening's TV to fit in an exercise session, or perhaps that an old friendship no longer serves you if you drink too much when you meet up.

Want it For a new beginning to be successful, it has to be something that you truly want. If you find yourself saying you 'should' or 'must' start meditating, then the motivation is not there. Dig deep about your reasons for wanting to change. Then, frame your goal in a sentence starting 'I want to ...' and mean it.

Start small Have your end-goal in mind, but set yourself a small target to begin with. If you want to do more exercise, for example, one session a week may be more achievable than a full-on gym workout every day. If you want to eat more healthily, pick a day in which you will have maximum nutrients — or perhaps choose to eat a healthy breakfast and not worry about the rest of the day for now.

Mark your achievement Have a way of recording your successes. This can be as simple as putting a tick on your calendar or you might use an app or a chart — whatever works for you.

Be kind Avoid all-or-nothing thinking. If you miss a day or a week, don't worry about it. Many studies show that self-criticism is counterproductive — when you feel bad about yourself, you are actually more likely to indulge in unhealthy behaviours. So, let yourself off and start again — another new beginning.

GENEROUS SPIRIT

'If nature has made you for a giver, your hands
are born open, and so is your heart.'

FRANCES HODGSON BURNETT, *A LITTLE PRINCESS*

According to research by psychologist Elizabeth Dunn, spending your money on other people gives you more pleasure than spending it on yourself. So one simple way to feel more content is to be a giver. Draw inspiration from St Nicholas, a bishop who lived in Myra, in modern-day Turkey, and was known for his kindness to children and generosity to the poor. According to legend, he dropped gold down the chimney of a poor man, thereby providing the necessary dowry for his daughters to marry. Thereafter any secret gifts were said to be from St Nicholas. His official feast day is 6 December – and it is on this day that many European children leave out shoes to be filled with treats.

Less is more There is no link between the amount of money a gift costs and the amount of pleasure that it gives. One of Dunn's experiments involved giving people $5 or $20 to spend on others – the happy boost was the same regardless of the sum involved.

It's the thought that counts Sentimental gifts tend to be more welcome than generic ones. Given the choice of a voucher for a favourite store or a framed photo of themselves with the giver, most people appreciated the personalized gift more.

Be aware The best gifts are those that speak to the recipient's likes and interests. Go shopping together and observe the sort of things they are drawn to. And if they mention something they are interested in, make an instant note of it.

CHAPTER FOUR:
PHILOSOPHERS, WRITERS & POETS

'Happiness resides not in possessions,
and not in gold, happiness
dwells in the soul.'

DEMOCRITUS

A LIFETIME'S WORK

'The activity of happiness must occupy an entire lifetime;
for one swallow does not a summer make.'

ARISTOTLE

Born in Greece around 384 BC, Aristotle is often held to be the greatest of the ancient Greek philosophers. Like thinkers throughout the ages, he realized that true happiness was not the same as enjoying sensual or material pleasures. While these could bring fleeting moments of joy, he believed that genuine contentment was a deeper and lasting state that can only result when we are living in accordance with our essential nature.

Eyes on the Prize
Aristotle was interested in the end purpose of things. He held that the goal of a knife is to cut things, the goal of medicine is good health – and that the goal of life is happiness. In Aristotle's view, the defining characteristic of a human being is the ability to reason. Thus, he argued, true joy can be experienced only by living in a way that allows a person to exercise reason. In his view, happiness requires each of us to stick to a kind of middle path, rather than veering from one extreme to the other: excessive behaviour (rage, self-indulgence, avarice) tends to lead to unhappiness both in the short and the long term. And the long term is what matters;

*'Happiness is the meaning and purpose
of life, the whole aim and
end of human existence.'*

ARISTOTLE

when Aristotle says that happiness is the aim and end of human
existence, he means contentment is a journey that can take a
lifetime to complete.

FINDING PURPOSE

'Let yourself be silently drawn by the stronger
pull of what you really love.'

RUMI

Keeping our long-term goals in mind can help us to make better choices in the short term — and ultimately allows us to live in a way that resonates with who we really are. This exercise is intended to help you dig deep and discover what truly makes you feel happy.

1. Take a pen and notebook and go into a quiet room. Leave your phone outside and switch off any other electronic devices.
2. Write 'My life purpose' at the top of a page and then start jotting down anything that comes to mind — words, phrases, sentences, paragraphs. Consider things you like to do, such as running, gardening, or writing.
3. Let yourself feel fine about whatever you write down. If 'being rich' comes up for you, write it down. However, try to think more deeply about what being rich would give you — a bigger house, say? Then think what that thing would give you … more space for your interests, perhaps, or the ability to host big parties? Keep going until you feel you have found the core appeal.

4. Whenever you write something that engenders a strong emotional response in you, put a circle around it.

5. Gift yourself the time for this exercise — spend at least twenty minutes on your initial list. Don't worry if you don't get an answer that feels 'right' — keep going, or take a break and return to the list when you have rested.

6. When you feel ready, look over what you have written — especially the words that you have ringed. Reflect on what this tells you about yourself; is there a link or a theme? Write a sentence or two on what your inner purpose is.

7. Consider ways to integrate your sense of purpose with your daily life. This may be taking the first steps towards a complete change of direction, or it could mean making more time for things that you love to do. For example, if you love to read, would it help to make a reading space in your home? If being outdoors seems to matter, then what opportunities can you create to do that?

8. Keep your notes somewhere safe and review them periodically to check that you are living in a way that resonates with what you feel your purpose is. Living with purpose is an ongoing exercise.

'*Adopt the pace of nature,*
her secret is patience.'

RALPH WALDO EMERSON

NATURAL INSTINCT

Ralph Waldo Emerson was a nineteenth-century American academic and essayist who led the spiritual movement transcendentalism. At its heart, transcendentalism held that people, like nature, were inherently good. Emerson taught that we can achieve happiness and fulfilment when we are self-reliant rather than depending on society and its institutions; and that people should develop their own understanding of the universe and God through direct communion with the natural world.

Back to Nature

The transcendentalist view was that human beings have lost their connection with nature and need to re-engage with it in order to understand the meaning of the universe and their place within it, and thus achieve happiness. Emerson's follower Henry David Thoreau took this lesson to its ultimate conclusion when he went to 'live life simply' in a hut on Emerson's land for two years. His book, *Walden*, in which he reflects on his experiment became an American classic and has been described as the most influential guide to happy living ever. One of the key lessons he took from his minimalist lifestyle was the joy that could come from watching events unfurl in their own natural way – in other words, by developing the patience embodied by all living things.

PRACTISE PATIENCE

Emerson and Thoreau inspired people to find solitude as well as patience by tuning into and appreciating their natural surroundings. For most of us there isn't a day that goes by without some disturbance or delay. If we practise tolerance during those times, we are more likely to live a life of calmness and contentment. However, it takes both emotional and thought ingenuity to master the art of acceptance. Here are some helpful tips to guide you toward a less stressful and more patient existence:

Recognize the benefits of patience It is no fun being a weather vane and reacting to every little bit of wind that comes our way. Instead, notice how nice it feels to be tranquil, centred and at ease. You can accomplish more and retain your energy for the important things when you are patient.

See your impatience as something internal We tend to externalize when things get tough, blaming our moods on long lines or noisy environments. Instead, check in with yourself and develop awareness of how impatience grows inside you. When you are able to notice your tolerance getting lower, you have a better chance to catch it on the way down and slowly bring it back up to calmness.

Manage your expectations When we are impatient, it is easy to let our 'shoulds' and 'ought tos' get the better of us. For example, 'he should know how to count out money', or 'she should be using the other lane if she is going to drive like that'. Remembering that people or situations don't operate according to a plan can help to raise your patience level.

Ask yourself if you have the power to change the difficulty or delay By recognizing that you are not capable of improving the situation, you move away from the impulse to fight or flight. Instead of watching the very thing that is testing your patience, try switching your attention to something more pleasing and witness your calmness grow.

See the humour If all else fails, think of something funny and give out a little chuckle. Doing so will help not only ease your inner tension, but it will make the time go by more enjoyably.

'Trees that are slow to grow bear
the best fruit.'

MOLIÈRE

ETERNAL STUDENT

'Prefer knowledge to wealth, for the one is transitory, the other perpetual.'

SOCRATES

S ocrates was the first thinker known to have stated that happiness is achievable by effort, rather than a gift willed by the gods. He believed that human beings could become happy by enjoying learning for its own sake and by educating themselves to associate pleasure with higher ideals. Modern research seems to back up his views: a study of more than 15,000 people in the UK found that people with a higher level of education tended to feel happier with life; and happiness experts often recommend learning something new as a way of boosting feelings of engagement and satisfaction.

Master something new The mind can be seen as a muscle, a part of us that needs exercise in order to stay at its peak and to promote feelings of well-being. Make learning an integral part of your life: study a language, take up an instrument or learn a new skill.

Watch and learn Make a point of watching quality documentaries: a study by the BBC and the University of California, Berkeley, found that viewing nature programmes increased feelings of awe, amusement and joy while reducing anxiety, fear and stress.

Read books! Several studies have found that reading reduces depression and boosts self-esteem and feelings of satisfaction. Research at the University of Liverpool found that reading not only increased overall life satisfaction, but can inspire us to make positive and life-changing decisions, such as looking for a new job, travelling or taking up a new hobby.

FULL-HEARTED LIVING

"Tis better to have loved and lost than never to have loved at all.'

ALFRED LORD TENNYSON

B ertrand Russell — mathematician, thinker and historian — wrote a wonderful book called *The Conquest of Happiness*. In that book, he identifies some of the 'causes of unhappiness'; the things that keep us from finding contentment in our daily lives. One of these, he says, is timidity around love and the fear of taking the plunge in relationships.

Dare to Love

Being in love is one of life's great and indescribable joys — and Russell points out that, once the first flames of passion have died down, there is much happiness to be had from the familiarity and companionship that comes from loving another person. All the small everyday pleasures — from meals to watching a movie or going for a walk by the sea — can be enhanced by being shared with another person whose personality and company you appreciate. Perhaps most importantly, love for another individual makes us less self-centred: our own troubles naturally seem less important and we care less about what the world thinks of us (or rather what we think the world thinks of us). All of these things tend to make us happier.

FULL ENGAGEMENT

*'Being loved by someone gives you strength, while loving
someone deeply gives you courage.'*

LAO TZU

When we love someone we make ourselves vulnerable. Our natural
human need to feel secure is therefore at odds with the equally
natural need to be loved and to love. Many of us hold back in
our relationships in order to protect ourselves from the pain of
rejection or loss. But this also means we hold ourselves back from
full engagement. Participating fully in a relationship doesn't mean
telling everything or expressing every feeling you have. But it does
mean being completely present and allowing vulnerability. Here
are six ways to deepen the level of intimacy in a relationship:

Connect and reconnect Make a point of saying a heartfelt hello
and goodbye to your loved one. Acknowledge your connection
at the moment you take your leave, and the moment you come
back together.

Gaze on If you are both willing, practise a mini-meditation by
sitting facing each other and making eye contact. Let your breathing
follow its natural rhythm as you gaze into each other's eyes for a
full minute (it's fine to blink). Be open to the emotions that arise
as you do this — you may laugh, feel awkward or experience a sense
of deep connection.

Be interested   Russell advocated living with 'zest' – being infinitely curious and interested and engaged in all aspects of daily routine. One simple way to introduce greater zest into your relationship is by continuing to try new experiences. A small thing such as taking a walk somewhere new, trying a different café to the one you usually visit or cooking a new recipe together can help create mini zest moments.

Lose the phone   Make a point of putting phones aside when you are with loved ones – in particular over dinner and in bed. In one American study, people who judged their partners to be overly dependent on their smartphones were less satisfied in their relationships than those with less tech-addicted partners.

Have date nights   This is familiar advice, but studies show that couples who make time for each other are happier overall.

Face up to loss   One great fear partners have is that they will not be able to cope if the relationship ends. Acknowledging to yourself that you would, in fact, be okay can conversely allow you to take greater risks in commitment.

THE SIMPLE LIFE

'A wise man is content with his lot, whatever it may be,
without wishing for what he has not.'

SENECA

The Stoics believed that a right attitude and self-control were key to maintaining inner contentment in the face of life's highs and lows. They held that it was possible to be happy whatever one's circumstances, and the varied backgrounds of some of the most famous Stoics seem to bear this out: Marcus Aurelius was an emperor, Epictetus was a slave, and the fortunes of Seneca roller coastered from wealth and power to humiliation and exile, and back again. Stoicism was a highly popular belief system for more than 500 years, and its message echoes that of many of other ancient philosophies.

A Dose of Difficulty

Seneca the Younger's prescription for contentment is to practise poverty and difficulty before one needs to. In *Letters from a Stoic*, addressed to a friend who had sought his advice, he wrote: 'It is precisely in times of immunity from care that the soul should toughen itself beforehand for occasions of greater stress'. He counsels a precise course of action: 'Set aside a certain number of days, during which you shall be content with the scantiest and cheapest fare, with coarse and rough dress, saying to yourself the while: "Is this the condition that I feared?" ... Endure all this for

three or four days at a time, sometimes for more, so that it may be a test of yourself instead of a mere hobby. Then, I assure you … you will leap for joy when filled with a pennyworth of food, and you will understand that a man's peace of mind does not depend upon Fortune; for, even when Fortune is angry, she grants enough for our needs.'

PARING DOWN NEEDS

We can apply Seneca's idea of practising poverty by introducing regular days of pared-back living into our week or month. This helps to build greater appreciation for all that one has, and also encourages us to reign in our expectations and demands.

1. Choose a set period over which you are going to practise pared-back living. It could be a single day in the week or – as Seneca advises – three or four days, perhaps each month or at the start of each new season.
2. Before you start, make a note of what a pared-back day means to you. Here are some ideas:
    ○ Refrain from using screens for all non-essential activities and, ideally, ban them altogether.
    ○ Spend no money. If you are at work, take your lunch from home.
    ○ Eat as simply as possible. You may want to eliminate caffeine, sugar, alcohol and any processed food from your diet; cut out any snacks, but eat normally at mealtime; or – if you are used to it – you may want to include fasting in your simplicity day.
    ○ Spend time outdoors in nature.
    ○ Make your shower a cold one.
    ○ Avoid chatty conversations, especially with people who create complications in your life.

GROWING APPRECIATION

Once you get into the routine of pared-back days, you
may find you start to exercise greater restraint and
greater appreciation at other times as well.

3. Write your pared-back days on your calendar or schedule
   and commit to doing them.
4. Use the additional hours and minutes that a pared-
   back day gives you to spend time in nature, meditate or
   engage in other simple activities that feel worthwhile.

TAKE NOTE

The great Russian novelist Leo Tolstoy used writing to explore human ambition and emotion. His greatest works, *Anna Karenina* and *War and Peace*, are populated with hundreds of characters who fall in love, fight for their lives, weep, laugh, grow... Tolstoy was a master of the sweeping historical panorama – battles and clashes of nations – but he could also imagine and articulate the innermost thoughts of, say, a teenage girl attending the ballet for the first time.

Keeping a Journal

Tolstoy spent his life examining his own soul, trying to find answers to the eternal questions of life and meaning, good and evil. At the age of eighteen he began writing a 'Journal of Daily Activities' in which he would note down each activity – including mealtimes and study – with the number of hours he intended to spend on each, and then would later make a note of how he had met his goals. His entries ranged from 'badly' or 'overslept' to a tick! Once he was world-famous, his daily entries were leaked like news reports – much to his fury. So he began to keep a separate and secret diary, which he hid down the leg of his tall Russian boot.

Tolstoy understood that we all need a private outlet for our innermost feelings, and countless modern studies confirm that journalling has a therapeutic effect and can help boost feelings of happiness and well-being.

WRITE IT OUT

Tolstoy, Isaac Newton, Oscar Wilde and Benjamin Franklin are just some of the eminent figures known for their practice of keeping journals as a tool of self-reflection. Today, there is mounting evidence that writing down your thoughts helps to reduce stress, as well as increasing emotional well-being and centring our minds. Cognitive behavioural therapists use journalling as a tool to help patients manage grief, lower emotional reactivity, track patterns, resolve internal dilemmas and witness their growth. Here is a brief guide to making the most of journalling:

1. Start by writing down your top three 'way of life' principles at the beginning of your new journal. This could be anything from approaching things with a positive frame of mind or practicing patience. Write whatever comes to mind and rings true for you.

2. At the end of the day, sit down with your journal. Think of a difficulty or upsetting feeling you have experienced. Write a brief paragraph about it — try not to censor yourself, but express yourself openly on the page.

3. Once you have finished your description, take a moment to reflect truthfully about how objective your perceptions have been about this feeling or problem? Note this down under your first paragraph.

4. Now turn to your 'way of life principles' at the front of your journal. How does your handling of this problem

align with these? Note down whether you are behaving in accordance with your core values, or if there could be a more beneficial way to think or act about this situation?

5. In three simple bullet points, answer the following questions in relation to your situation:
    ◉ How could it be a learning experience for you, a chance to change and grow?
    ◉ What is the worst thing that could possibly come about because of this?
    ◉ Have you acted considerately to yourself and others in this situation?

6. End your journalling with how you might flip this feeling or problem to make it more meaningful, relieving or pleasant for you or others.

'Seize the moments of happiness, love and be loved! That is the only reality in the world, all else is folly.'

TOLSTOY, *WAR AND PEACE*

POSITIVE THINKING

'The more a man meditates upon good thoughts, the better
will be his world and the world at large.'

CONFUCIUS

Negative thinking can become a habit that impacts on our general attitude to the world, our mood and our ability to enjoy life. So, bear the words of the ancient Chinese philosopher Confucius in mind and make a conscious effort to think good thoughts. Here are four ways to foster positivity:

1. When you speak, use positive words and phrases. Replace 'I can't' with 'I am going to try', or perhaps 'I choose not to'. Instead of facing 'difficulty' try to see the 'challenge'... or even an 'opportunity'.

2. Pick a positive phrase that sums up how you want to feel. Perhaps 'I choose to feel joy today'. Write it on a sticky note and place it somewhere you are bound to catch sight of it in the morning. Repeat it to yourself at intervals during the day – with focus and real feeling. You have to mean it in order to believe it!

3. When you notice that you are thinking negatively, don't use it as an opportunity to berate yourself. A thought is just a thought. Simply notice it and let it go. Or try visualizing a big red STOP sign before redirecting your thoughts to something more positive.